FAITH
IN FRIENDSHIP

My Friend Is
Hindu

by Khadija Ejaz

PURPLE TOAD
PUBLISHING

FAITH

IN FRIENDSHIP

My Friend Is Buddhist
My Friend Is Christian
My Friend Is Hindu
My Friend Is Jewish
My Friend Is Muslim

For all the Indian movies that brought Hindu symbolism into my very Muslim childhood in the Middle East—
Khadija Ejaz

Printing 1 2 3 4 5 6 7 8 9

Publisher's Cataloging-in-Publication Data
Ejaz, Khadija.
    My friend Is Hindu. / written by Khadija Ejaz.
        p. cm.
Includes timeline, further reading, bibliography and glossary.
            ISBN 9781624691089
1. Hinduism—Juvenile literature. 2. Hinduism—North America. I. Series: Faith in Friendship
  BL1100 2015
  294.5
                                            2014945181

eBook ISBN: 9781624691096

Contents

Narasimha, the lion avatar of Vishnu, erupts out of a pillar.

New Jersey Hindus

The end was near for Prahlad. The young man had defied his father, the demon-king Hiranyakashyap, by worshiping the god Vishnu. That had made proud Hiranyakashyap very angry. He was an *asura*—a demon—and he despised the gods. Had he not been granted immortality by the god Brahma himself? No god, man, demon, or animal could kill him. He was better than the gods, and his son's devotion to Vishnu drove him mad with rage. He had ordered his soldiers to tie Prahlad to a pillar, and they were soon going to behead him.

"Watch this!" I told Cameron. This was my favorite part of the cartoon. We were in my house in the living room, sitting cross-legged in front of the television. Cameron was staring at the screen, mouth open.

The pillar exploded, and out of the dust and debris leaped Narasimha, the lion avatar of

Vishnu. He had the head of a lion, and the body of a man. He was very muscular, and each of his many arms ended with powerful claws. What a fearsome sight! Hiranyakashyap's soldiers were terrified, and they ran off in all directions.

Cameron jumped. "Yikes!" he said.

With a deafening roar, Narasimha grabbed Hiranyakashyap and laid him out on his lap. He tore into the demon-king's torso with his claws. Hiranyakashyap the tyrant was now dead, and Prahlad was safe. Vishnu had rescued his devotee and restored *rita,* the cosmic order, once again.

"Wow, Arjun," Cameron said as he turned toward me. "I've never seen anything like this!"

Cameron and I had known each other for only a few hours, but we got along really well. His mother had brought him with her when she came to visit my mother here in our new house in Jersey City, New Jersey. Our

Arjun (left) and Cameron became friends while watching cartoons in Arjun's living room. Cameron also met the rest of Arjun's family that day, including his father, mother, and twin sisters.

This is Arjun's father. Doesn't he have an inviting smile?

mothers were out on the patio. They work together in the same office.

My mother's name is Smriti Gupta, and she is a web designer. She is from Trinidad and Tobago but is of Indian descent. My father, Rishi Gupta, is a psychiatrist. He is from India. My sisters Puja and Aarti are fifteen years old and twins. I call them both *didi,* which is Hindi for "elder sister." If I had an older brother, I would have called him *bhai.* I am eleven years old and attend sixth grade—just like Cameron.

My family has been living in New Jersey for only a few weeks. We used to live in Queens in New York. That's where my sisters and I were born. I miss my old school and my friends in Queens, but my family doesn't have to drive too far to visit them. And Jersey City, like Queens, has a very large South Asian community, so we can still buy our groceries and traditional clothes at the many shops here and stay connected to the Hindu community. My family has already made new friends. We met a lot of them on Holi at the Hindu temple here.

Cameron tapped me on my shoulder.

"Hey, Arjun," he said. "I'm still thinking about the story of Narasimha. How did he kill Hiranya . . . Hiranya . . ."

"Hiranyakashyap" (hih-RUN-yuh-kash-yip).

"Yes, Hiranyakashyap. I thought the demon-king was immortal and that no man or animal could kill him."

"That's true," I said. "But Vishnu was clever. His avatar Narasimha was neither man nor animal. That is how he was able to kill Hiranyakashyap."

"What's an avatar? Isn't that a character you make of yourself in videogames? And the name of a famous movie?"

"You're right," I said. "The name of that movie comes from the ancient Sanskrit word *avatar*. According to Hindu mythology, the gods can choose to live on earth in human form. Their human incarnations are called avatars."[1]

Cameron looked confused. "And you're Hindi?"

I laughed. People confuse the words *Hindi* and *Hindu* all the time. Hindi is the national language of India and has roots in an ancient language called Sanskrit. A Hindu, on the other hand, is a person who follows the ancient Vedic traditions of South Asia. Almost all of the world's Hindus live in that region.[2] Most people use the word *Hinduism* to refer to South Asia's Vedic religious heritage, but the Hindus themselves prefer to call it *sanatana dharma,* "the eternal religion."

"Alright, so you're a Hindu, then," said Cameron. He stressed on the word *Hindu* and looked pleased with himself for getting it right.

"You know, Cameron, you ought to meet my grandmother," I said. "She knows a lot of stories from Hindu mythology." I was talking about my *dadi,* my father's mother, Lakshmi Gupta. She lives in New Delhi in India but often visits us in the United States. My *dada*—her husband and my grandfather—passed away a couple of years ago in India, and we have been trying to convince her to move in with us ever since. Dada's photo hangs high up on a wall in our home. We keep it draped with a garland made of marigolds.

My late grandfather. We all miss him.

"You're in luck," I said. "Lakshmi *dadi* arrives in a week, and she will stay with us for a month. You must meet her and ask her to tell you some stories. I will tell her about you over the phone myself!"

I heard our front door open and recognized the voices of my father and my sisters. "My *didis* are back from their dance class," I said. My sisters have been learning Indian classical dances like Bharatanatyam and Kathak for many years. I attend music classes myself. I am learning how to play the sitar and the tabla. Many Hindu children spend years studying these ancient art forms, and they start at a very young age. In Hindu culture, dance and music are thought to be a form of *puja*

The sitar played by famous Indian musician Ravi Shankar. He is the father of singers Nora Jones and Anoushka Shankar.

(worship), and our *bhakti* (devotion) pleases the gods.[3] Many classical dances act out stories from Hindu mythology.

My father and sisters entered the living room where Cameron and I were still sitting on the floor. Puja and Aarti *didi* are identical twins, and today, they were wearing matching Indian Punjabi shalwar suits. They both wore their long, black hair in thick braids that dangled down their backs. So does our mother.

My father smiled at us. *"Namaste,"* he said to Cameron with his palms joined together in front of him. This traditional Hindu greeting means, "I acknowledge the divine in you."[4] Cameron introduced himself, and my sisters, who by now had settled onto the couch, said hello to him.

"Ma and Mrs. Parker are on the patio," I said. "We were just watching the Hindu mythology cartoons that we bought from the Indian store last week."

"Did you like the cartoons, Cameron?" my father asked. Cameron nodded. "Arjun, *beta,*" my father said to me. *Beta* is Hindi for "son." "Why

My bedroom is just as messy as any other kid's. Cameron will have a hard time sorting through story books here. We'll have to pretend we're on a treasure hunt!

don't you lend Cameron some of your story books on Hindu mythology? I think he'll enjoy reading them."

What a great idea!

"Come on, Cameron," I said as I rose to my feet. "Let's go to my room. I'll show you all my books, and you can pick the ones you like."

Aarti *didi* spoke up. "Arjun, did you offer Cameron any refreshments?"

"Yes," Puja *didi* chimed in. "Don't forget what *dadi* says—*atithi devo bhava.*"

"What does that mean?" Cameron asked.

My father smiled his usual smile that we all love so much. "It's a line from one of our Hindu scriptures," he said. "It's Sanskrit, and it means that the guest is God."

Welcome to our home, Cameron!

A World Religion

With around one billion followers worldwide, Hinduism is the third most popular religion in the world today (after Christianity and Islam, respectively). That's about 15 percent of the world's population.

Hindus form less than 1 percent of the American population, but much of their culture is now part of mainstream America. Words like *guru* and *yoga* have become part of everyday vocabulary, and many Americans are familiar with Hindu concepts like reincarnation and karma. Not too many people outside the Hindu community, though, know much about the Hindu religion. Most people assume that all Hindus are from India, or that all Indians are Hindus. Maybe they can be forgiven for their assumption because the reality of the Hindu world is only slightly different.

India is a secular democracy which was formed as recently as 1947, and an overwhelming 94 percent of the worldwide Hindu population lives there. Eight out of every ten people in India are Hindu. India also has one of the largest populations of Muslims in the world. Christians, Buddhists, Sikhs, Jains, Zoroastrians, and Jews also strongly influence Indian culture, but given India's large share of the global Hindu population, it is easy to see why many people equate India (and India only) with Hinduism. Nepal and Bangladesh have the next largest share of the world's Hindus, but only at 2 percent and 1 percent, respectively. Almost all of the world's Hindus live in the Asia-Pacific region, and only 1 percent live elsewhere.[5]

A Hindu Asian woman deeply immersed in prayer

Arjun's mother always wears her mangal sutra—the long gold-and-black chain around her neck.

All Roads Lead to India

Ma sometimes absentmindedly plays with her *mangal sutra*. She wears the necklace as a sign of being a married Hindu woman, the way other women in America wear a wedding ring. It had been a few weeks since I first met Cameron. Today he had returned to spend the day with me and had ended up talking to Ma. She stroked the black beads of her necklace as she told him the story of her great-great-grandfather.

"He came to Trinidad as an indentured laborer in 1850," she said. "Slavery had been abolished in 1834, but the British Empire still needed cheap labor to work in the sugar fields of Trinidad. Thousands of indentured laborers from British India were shipped to places like Fiji, Mauritius, Jamaica, and Trinidad. Many of them stayed on."

"Your great-great-grandfather was a Hindu?" Cameron said. Ma nodded.

"Yes, he was. He was a poor farmer from North India. He never went back to India but married

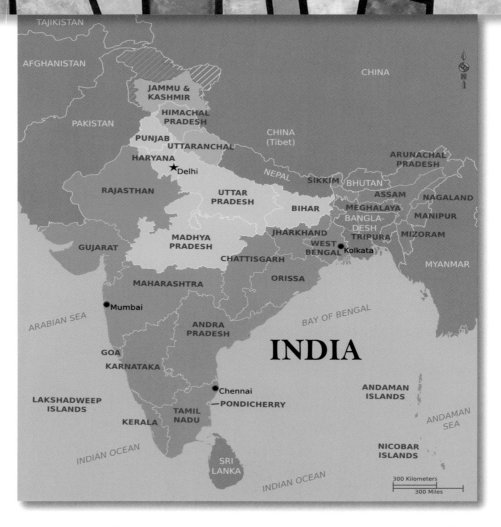

another Indian in Trinidad and settled there. I had never been to India until after I got married. My first visit to South Asia, the birthplace of Hindu tradition, helped me understand where I came from and what I believe in."

The history of *sanatana dharma* is very closely tied to the history of India. Ma began to tell Cameron about how the word *Hindu* was originally a geographic term that was used to refer to the people who lived across the Indus river. The Indus now flows through Tibet, India, and Pakistan. The ancient Sanskrit name of the river was Sindhu, and the Persians called it Hindu. In Latin, the river is called Indus.

Over time, people began to use the word *Hindu* to refer to the unique yet diverse religious beliefs of the people of South Asia. When the British

colonized that region, they grouped all the traditions of the Hindus under the term *Hinduism*, but the Hindus themselves still call it *sanatana dharma*.

"The word *India* comes from *Indoi*," Ma said, "which is what the Greeks called the people of the Indus. India is also called Hindustan—'the land of the Hindus'—and Bharat, after a famous king in Hindu mythology."

India's terrain also found its way into Hindu mythology. The snow-capped Himalaya are believed to be the home of the gods, like Mount Olympus was for the ancient Greeks. Even today, the Himalaya are home to many important Hindu pilgrimage sites. They inspired Meru, the mountain at the center of the Hindu universe.

"Did you read the story of the Ganga River in my books, Cameron?" I asked.

"I did," Cameron replied. "I read about how the earth had gone dry and how the gods asked the divine river Ganga to descend into the mortal world. The gods were worried that her strong waters would destroy the world, so the god Shiva let her flow to the earth through his long, wild hair and eased her powerful current."

"That's right," Ma said. "Today we know that the Ganga originates in the Himalaya; its source is a glacier called Gangotri."

The Ganga is so important to the Hindus that they call it *Ma* (mother). They believe that the waters of the river can wash away one's sins. Hindus are cremated after they die, and many of them have their ashes scattered into the Ganga. That is what we did with my grandfather's ashes, too.

"Mrs. Gupta," Cameron said, "who founded Hin—I mean, *sanatana dharma*?"

"*Sanatana dharma* doesn't have any one founder," Ma said. "In fact, it isn't even a religion but rather a family of religions."[1]

Cameron blinked. Ma understood that he was confused.

"Think of Hinduism this way," Ma said. "Judaism, Christianity, and Islam are different religions, but they all share a common philosophy which originated in the Middle East near the Jordan river. Let's call this philosophy Jordanism."[2]

Ma then told Cameron to think of Hinduism as the philosophy that arose around the Hindu (Sindhu) River. Many religions—including Buddhism, Jainism, and Sikhism—were founded on this philosophy.

"Hindu traditions have many sources," Ma said. "Some go back so far in history that no one knows how they started. They have been passed down to us through *rishis* (sages) and *acharyas* (teachers). In the beginning, *sanatana dharma* was purely ritualistic, but it became more personal and spiritual over time. Its roots can be found in the Indus Valley civilization and India's Vedic Period."

Ma took Cameron back all the way to 3000 BCE to the time of the Indus Valley civilization. It is also called the Sindhu Sarasvati civilization after a mythical river in the Hindu scriptures. At its peak, this civilization covered an area larger than modern Europe. These people traded with people in ancient Egypt and Mesopotamia.[3] Scholars can't read their writing yet, but they believe that many traditions of the modern Hindus originated there. Its people worshipped a mother goddess, nature, and a deity that eventually became the god Shiva. Some historians think that the large baths they found at this civilization's ruins were meant for religious bathing.

The Helmand River in Afghanistan. Some believe that this is the origin of the myth of the Sarasvati River from the Hindu scriptures.

"Then came the Aryans," Ma said. "They were a nomadic race from Central Asia that migrated into what is now northern India around 1500 BCE, and they brought the knowledge of the Vedas with them." The Vedas are the oldest and most important scriptures of the Hindus. There are four of them—the Rig Veda, the Sama Veda, the

Yajur Veda, and the Atharva Veda.

"Have you read the Vedas?" Cameron asked me. I shook my head.

"Most Hindus haven't," I said. "The Vedas are in Sanskrit, and only the most scholarly Hindus know the language now."

"Yes," Ma said. "The Hindu priests have always been the caretakers and interpreters of our scriptures. In fact, over time, they became so strict and powerful that at one point in history some people rebelled against their authority. Two of those reform movements survive as Buddhism and Jainism today."

A Rig Vedic manuscript in Sanskrit. The Rig Veda is one of the oldest religious texts in use today.

Hindu scriptures are categorized as either *shruti* ("that which is revealed") or *smriti* ("that which is remembered"). *Shruti* texts generally outrank the *smriti* and include the Vedas and their commentaries, like the Aranyakas, Brahmanas, and Upanishads. The Vedangas and Itihasas, which include the epics and the Puranas, are only some of the hundreds of *smriti* texts.

"The Vedic people thought fire linked the worlds of the humans and the gods," Ma said. "They performed fire ceremonies called *yagnas* and used an intoxicant called soma. Vedic rituals also emphasized social responsibilities. Some practices from the time of the Indus Valley civilization were absorbed into Vedic beliefs."

The ancient world knew the Hindus for their wealth and their advances in science and art. Hindu culture flourished across South Asia under various

The Angkor Wat temple complex in Angkor, Cambodia. It was built by the Khmer king Suryavarman II in the early twelfth century as part of the capital of his empire. The complex was dedicated to the god Vishnu. Angkor Wat means "City of Temples."

rulers who traded with other civilizations. Parts of Southeast Asia were colonized by powerful Hindu rulers from southern India who helped spread *sanatana dharma* and particularly Buddhism to that part of the world.[4]

Ma told Cameron about how she one day plans on visiting Cambodia to see the famous Hindu-Buddhist temple of Angkor Wat. It is the largest religious complex in the world and is a legacy of India's colonial past. The complex was built as a dedication to Vishnu, and its design represents the mythical Mount Meru.

Cameron was fascinated. Ma is a great storyteller! He listened to her as she told him more about Hindu history and how its culture evolved in South Asia with the arrival of the Muslims and the Christian Europeans. Hindu culture both absorbed and influenced the philosophies of Islam and Christianity, and it continues to adapt itself to life in the modern world wherever it is observed. I think my mother is proof of that.

Rewriting History

Hindus have always been touchy about the Aryan Invasion Theory, and modern scholars, too, suspect its intentions. They believe it to be a legacy of the colonial era when non-white culture was regularly trivialized by white, Christian Europe.[5]

The Aryan Invasion Theory was first proposed in the late nineteenth century by the German linguist Max Müller. He said that the people of South Asia, Persia, and Europe had common ancestors who came from Central Asia, and that they originally spoke Sanskrit. Müller called these ancestors "Aryans," from a word that the Vedas use to refer to a certain group of people. *Aryan* is Sanskrit for "noble."

The Hindus, however, have always believed that Sanskrit was from South Asia, and they disagreed with Müller, who said that it had been brought over from Central Asia by migrating Aryans. They believed Müller's motivations to be racist because he rejected the possibility that a culture as ancient and sophisticated as the Aryans could have non-white origins. The German dictator Adolf Hitler (among others) would go on to use this idea of a superior, white race to devastating ends.

Also, many European scholars at the time were devout Christians who believed that the world had been created around 4000 BCE. Native Hindu texts estimated their traditions to be much older. When faced with this dilemma, European historians adjusted the dates of Hindu traditions to hundreds of years later than the Hindus believed them to have occurred. Modern scholars are now re-examining these dates.

Max Müller

This is Arjun's grandmother. Isn't she lovable?

One Soul, Many Lives

"Did you know that I chose Arjun's name for him?"

Lakshmi *dadi* had arrived! She had been in the United States for a week when Cameron came over to meet her. I had told him so much about her. Cameron had been surprised that she was fluent in English. India has the world's largest population of non-native English speakers, after all, and Dadi had been a teacher for most of her life.

Dadi's white cotton sari rustled as she sat down at the dining table with a cup of tea. Cameron and I snacked on some sweets that she had brought from India. Dadi has worn white clothes since she became a widow. White is the color of mourning, or unhappiness, to the Hindus.

"Arjun is the name of the warrior hero in the Bhagavad Gita," Dadi said. The Bhagavad Gita is one of the most accessible holy books of the Hindus. This is the text that most ordinary Hindus

A representation of the battleground of Kurukshetra as described in the Bhagavad Gita. The god Krishna, who is usually depicted with blue skin, is seen holding the reins of Arjun's chariot, whom he is counseling at a moment of personal religious crisis.

turn to for moral and spiritual guidance. In India, Hindus swear on it in court the way that Christians do on the Bible in the United States.[1]

Bhagavad Gita means "Song of the Lord," and it contains poetic dialogue between Arjun and the god Krishna. It is actually part of a much larger Hindu epic called the Mahabharata, but it is considered a book in its own right. Dadi knows the story of the divine song well.

"Arjun was seized with doubt at the battleground of Kurukshetra," she said. "He was going to war against his cousins, and he felt despair at the thought of all the bloodshed that was going to follow. He confided his fears to Krishna, who was serving as his charioteer. Krishna consoled him with his divine knowledge. He spoke to him about *sanatana dharma* and reminded Arjun that, as a warrior, it was his dharma to take up arms. Ultimately, Krishna convinced Arjun not to abandon his cause and to fight for what was right."

Dharma, or religious duty, is very important to the Hindus. It tells them how to act according to their place in society. Hindu society is divided into classes that are called varnas. These were originally flexible and meant to organize society by occupation, but over time they came to be determined by birth. The word varna means "color," and some scholars believe that the lighter-skinned Aryans created the system by placing themselves higher up in this system and the darker natives of South Asia farther down.[2]

The four varnas are those of the Brahmin (priest), Kshatriya (warrior), Vaishya (trader), and Shudra (laborer), and there are numerous subclasses called jatis under them. Jati means "birth." Some Hindus fall below the Shudras and hence outside the class system, and today they are called Dalits. Our scriptures tell us that the varnas were created from Purusha, the cosmic giant. The Brahmins came from his mouth, the Kshatriyas from his arms, the Vaishyas from his thighs, and the Shudras from his feet.

The lives of Brahmin, Kshatriya, and Vaishya men are each also divided into four stages called ashramas. Each stage is about 25 years long. They are, in order, the stages of the brahmacharya (student), grihastha (householder), vanaprastha (retiree), and sanyasa (renunciate). So crucial are the varna and ashrama in determining one's dharma, that sanatana dharma is also called varnashrama dharma.

The life of a Hindu is also marked by sixteen rites of passage called samskaras. Marriage and having children are very important in Hindu society, and the earliest samskaras are performed while the child is still in the womb. The last samskara is performed when a person dies. Some intermediate samskaras include the naming ceremony, betrothal, and marriage.

"Dadi," Cameron said. That made my grandmother smile. "Tell me more about Krishna."

Lord Krishna was a famous king in Hindu mythology, and he is considered to be an avatar of Vishnu. The story of another avatar of Vishnu's can be found in an epic called the Ramayana, which narrates the adventures of the king Rama. Most Hindus believe that Vishnu had ten avatars. They also believe that Gautama Buddha, the founder of Buddhism, was one of them.

"Vishnu is only one of the Hindu gods, Cameron," I said. "There are many more. Some say as many as 330 million![3] The same deity can have different names depending on where it is worshipped. The biggest temples are dedicated to the most popular gods, but other more local gods may be worshipped at the village level."

Dadi sipped her tea delicately. "At the end of the day, it is important to remember that all our gods are different forms of the one true god who is the source of everything. We call that god Brahman."

Brahman is also called Ishvar or Bhagwaan. Dadi continued to speak.

"Brahman is pure consciousness and has no physical form. The modern world believes that consciousness arises from matter. *Sanatana dharma* tells us the opposite, that matter comes from consciousness."

The Hindus believe that every living thing—a person, an animal, and even an insect—has a soul called an *atman,* and that the *atman* comes from Brahman. The *atman* is eternal and without form, but it takes physical form on Earth and lives out many lives. This cycle of reincarnation is called *samsara.* If the *atman* lives according to its *dharma*, then it will create good karma and be born at a higher level in the next life. If not, it will reincarnate as a lower life form. The goal of every *atman* is to move so high up the rebirth ladder that it breaks free from *samsara.* When this happens, the *atman* gains *moksha* (freedom) and returns to Brahman.

"This world is *maya,* an illusion," Dadi said. "And only enlightenment can help us see through the illusion. Our scriptures tell us that enlightenment can be achieved through knowledge, deeds, devotion, or yoga."

Dadi told Cameron about the *trimurti,* which is the trinity of the gods Brahma, Vishnu, and Shiva. These are the most popular gods in the Hindu pantheon. Brahma creates worlds, Vishnu maintains them, and Shiva destroys them and ends the cycle of time so that Brahma can start it again. The Hindus believe that time is eternal and runs in circles. Each circle is 4,320,000 years long and goes through four *yugas* (ages). The world is at

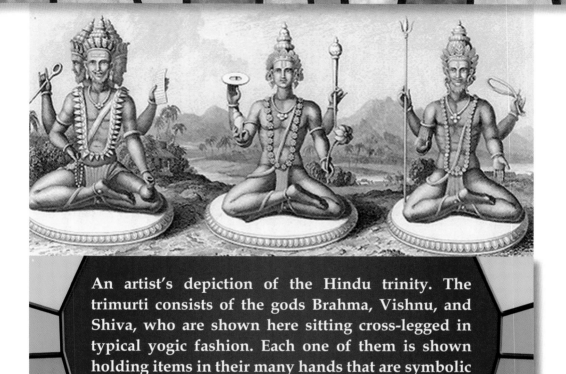

An artist's depiction of the Hindu trinity. The trimurti consists of the gods Brahma, Vishnu, and Shiva, who are shown here sitting cross-legged in typical yogic fashion. Each one of them is shown holding items in their many hands that are symbolic of their powers and aspects of their personalities.

its most harmonious in the first *yuga,* and it declines into complete choas by the last one.

"Our world is currently going through its last *yuga,*" Dadi said. "It began around 3000 BCE when Lord Krishna died. This age is called the *Kali yuga,* and it will last for 432,000 years, after which Shiva will bring this world to an end."

"My family worships Lord Krishna," I told Cameron, "but *sanatana dharma* gives us the freedom to worship whichever god that we feel drawn to. That deity becomes our *ishta devata,* our personally desired divinity. I like music, and so I also pray to Saraswati, the goddess of knowledge and the arts. My sisters do, too."

Saraswati is Brahma's consort. Dadi is named after Vishnu's consort, Lakshmi, who represents prosperity. Ma believes in women's rights and so has a personal preference for Durga, the powerful consort of Shiva. Durga is the fierce form of the milder goddess Parvati. When Durga gets really

The goddess Kaali. This fierce goddess is particularly revered by those who practice tantric Hindu rituals.

angry at the injustice in the world, she becomes Kaali. Kaali is terrifying! She has dark skin, wild hair, and she wears a skirt of severed arms and a garland made of severed heads. Her long red tongue hangs from her mouth dripping blood.

Hindu beliefs are as complex and diverse as they are old, but most Hindus can be thought of as devotees of Vishnu, Shiva, or Shakti. In a way, these groups make up the Hindu religions that arose from *sanatana dharma*.[4] Vaishnavites worship Vishnu in all his forms, and they form the largest Hindu religion. Devotees of Shiva are called Shaivites. Shakti is the feminine version of the ultimate reality; the tridevi (the consorts of the *trimurti*) are her various forms. Other Hindu gods represent the forces of nature, such as Surya (sun), Vayu (wind), Indra (thunder), and Agni (fire).

Dadi finished her tea and leaned back in her chair. "My late husband was a good man," she said. "The gods were always on his mind. Our last thoughts influence our next life, so I'm sure that he must have attained moksha and become one with Brahman."

Approaching the Gods

Hindu worship is very personal and revolves around *murtis* (statues). Most Hindus perform *pujas* at home in a special section of their house where they can place pictures or *murtis* of their favorite religious figures. *Murtis* are strictly designed according to Hindu scriptures, and they are believed to contain the spirit of the deity they represent. They allow devotees to perform *darshan*, which is the act of being in the presence of a god. *Darshan* is central to Hindu worship. Hindus believe that not only does darshan allow them to see their deity, but it permits the deity to see them as well.

Hindu temples, or *mandirs*, are not meant for sermons but are intended to house the gods. They are built according to cosmic diagrams called *mandalas* that represent the Hindu universe. At the heart of the temple is a shrine called the *garbhagriha* ("womb chamber"), which is where the *murti* is placed. Only Brahmin priests can enter this shrine. They tend to the *murti* by performing numerous *pujas* all day long so that the gods stay happy.

During a *puja*, the *murti* is treated like a royal guest. Devotees come barefooted and announce their presence to the deity by ringing a bell. They may also walk around the shrine or temple clockwise. The *murti* is bathed and decorated, and an *aarti* is performed in which light and fragrance are offered to the *murti*. Food, flowers, and money are also offered for blessings and are later consumed by the devotees as *prasad*.

Offerings of sound are made in the form of devotional songs called *bhajans* or Vedic verses called *mantras*. Sound is important to the Hindus—they believe that the names of the gods and other spiritual masters have special powers. The word *Om* is believed to be the sound of creation and is Brahman in sound form.[5]

A Hindu man performing a *puja* for the god Shiva.

The garden of a typical *ashram* in India.

Hindus in History

A couple of weeks later, Cameron's mother dropped him off at our home while she and Ma went out shopping together. The two of us found our way to the living room where this time we were joined by my sisters. We were watching the American movie *Eat, Pray, Love*. Parts of it had been filmed at an *ashram* in India. *Ashrams* are communities where Hindus can go on spiritual retreats or take part in religious activities.

The movie had made big news in India. I remember reading all about it when it was being filmed. What made even bigger news was when its leading American actress Julia Roberts announced that she had become a Hindu. The movie was based on a book by the American author Elizabeth Gilbert, who had adopted the way of *sanatana dharma* as well.

Hindu society originally did not accept converts or allow people to leave it. For a very long time, it was believed that one could only become a Hindu by being born into a Hindu family. Some people like to use the word as it was originally used in the geographic sense, while others believe that anyone who accepts the authority of the Vedas is a Hindu. The Indian constitution regards Buddhists, Jains, and Sikhs as Hindus as well.[1]

"Are there any other famous Hindus in America?" Cameron asked us.

Puja *didi* reached out for her smart phone and opened an Internet browser window. She pulled up a picture of a man and showed it to Cameron.

"Do you know him?" she said.

Cameron peered at the screen of her phone. "I think I do," he said. "I've seen his face on some of my mother's books. Oh, what is his name . . . I can't remember."

Deepak Chopra

The man's name was Deepak Chopra. He is a world-famous motivational speaker and is of Indian descent. In fact, he was born and raised in New Delhi, which is where my father is from. Chopra came to America as a doctor, and that is how he made his living for many years. He later turned to alternative medicine, specifically the ancient Hindu science of the Ayurveda, which started him on the path to becoming a modern spiritual guru. Chopra is the author of many self-help books, and most people first came to know about him from his regular appearances on *The Oprah Winfrey Show.*

"Have you heard of the Maharishi Mahesh Yogi?" Aarti *didi* asked Cameron. He shook his head. My sister kept talking.

"Well, have you heard of the Beatles?"

"The band from Liverpool, England?" Cameron said immediately. "My whole family loves their music!"

"Most people in the West know Maharishi Mahesh Yogi because of his association with the Beatles," Aarti *didi* said. "He

The Maharishi Mahesh Yogi in 1978. Maharishi and Yogi are titles, which mean "Great Seer" and "practitioner of yoga," respectively.

was a spiritual guru, and the Beatles once traveled to India to see him in the Himalayan town of Rishikesh. Have you heard of Rishikesh? It is called the 'Yoga Capital of the World.' The Maharishi also founded the Transcendental Meditation movement."

Puja *didi* likes the Beatles, too. Her favorite Beatles song is "Hey, Jude"—we've heard her sing it loudly in the shower many times! She looked up another picture on her phone and showed it to Cameron.

"That's George Harrison," she said. "He was one of the Beatles and was the man who introduced the band to the Maharishi. He later became a devotee of Paramahansa Yogananda, who was one of the first Hindu gurus to become famous in the United States. His book, *Autobiography of a Yogi,* is still popular in the West."

Puja *didi* told Cameron that George Harrison ultimately became part of the International Society for Krishna Consciousness (ISKCON), which is more commonly known as the Hare Krishna Mission. ISKCON is a *Vaishnavite sampradaya* (religious lineage) that was founded in New York City in 1966 by AC Bhaktivedanta Swami Prabhupada. ISKCON believes that *bhakti* can

George Harrison in India in 1996. Harrison had a number 1 hit with "My Sweet Lord," which was a song about his belief in the god Krishna.

lead to *moksha*.[2] It models its practices on Chaitanya Mahaprabhu, who was an Indian saint from the sixteenth century. Another famous figure in the *bhakti* world was the female saint Mirabai. She lived at the same time as Mahaprabhu and composed many devotional songs to Krishna.

Harrison also became a vegetarian. Not all Hindus are vegetarian, but many of them are. Some Hindus don't even eat eggs. *Sanatana dharma* stresses ahimsa (nonviolence), and many Hindus believe that that philosophy should be extended toward animals as well.

In ancient times, however, animals were offered as sacrifices to the Hindu deities, and although the practice has mostly died out, some Hindu sects still follow it. Certain *varnas* and *jaatis* were known to eat meat at various times in history. Many still do. At the end of the day, though, even a meat-eating Hindu will not eat beef or harm a cow because that animal is considered sacred by all Hindus.

My father once told me the reason behind this belief: ancient Hindus lived in villages (as many do today) where cows are an important part of the economy. Cows gave nutritious milk and helped plow the fields, and their dung was used as fertilizer.[3] Cows were so important that they served as a measure of a family's wealth. This is similar to how the Semites in the arid Middle East felt about their camels.

My sisters know a lot about American pop culture, and they told Cameron about other famous Hindus like M. Night Shyamalan, the famous Indian-American director who made horror movies like *The Sixth Sense* and *Signs;* Jhumpa Lahiri, an award-winning British-born Indian-American author; and Russell Brand, the British comedian.

"One of the most famous Hindus in the world is Mohandas Karamchand Gandhi," I said. "You must have heard of him. He was an important personality of the Indian freedom struggle against the British Empire."

In modern times, Gandhi is remembered as a spiritual leader who relied on his Hindu beliefs for guidance. He was born in British India, but he studied law in London and spent many years practicing in South Africa. It was only after experiencing discrimination between the white and non-white people there that he decided to return to the land of his birth and join the movement for Indian independence.

Gandhi felt strongly for the downtrodden, and he worked hard to improve the conditions of the Dalits, who were then called the Untouchables. Gandhi called them Harijans, which means "Children of God." In a land that suffered from Hindu-Muslim violence, he stressed harmony between the religions. His techniques of nonviolent resistance were based on *ahimsa,* and they inspired many people around the world, including the American civil rights activist Martin Luther King, Jr., and South Africa's Nelson Mandela.

Mahatma Gandhi underwent long fasts as a form of social protest.

Filmmaker Satyajit Ray who directed the world-renowned "Apu Trilogy."

"In India, Gandhi is remembered as Bapu and Mahatma," I said. "*Bapu* means 'father,' and *Mahatma* means 'Great Soul.'"

"Let me see if I can think of some other famous Hindus from India," Aarti *didi* said. She counted on her fingers as she told Cameron about Amartya Sen, a Nobel Prize–winning economist; Mahesh Bhupathi, a famous tennis player; Mira Nair, a director who made a film out of Jhumpa Lahiri's book, *The Namesake;* Satyajit Ray, another famous movie director; and Sachin Tendulkar, a famous cricketer.

"Don't forget Rabindranath Tagore," Puja *didi* said. "He was a gifted poet from India, and also the first Asian to win the Nobel Prize. He composed India's national anthem."

"And VS Naipaul," I added. "He is a Nobel Prize–winning writer. Have you read any of his books? He was born in Britain, but his family was from Trinidad and Tobago. Naturally, he is our mother's favorite writer!"

Writer VS Naipaul. His ancestors came from India as indentured laborers.

Art Versus Blasphemy

Controversy followed the Indian Muslim painter Maqbool Fida Husain wherever he went. He particularly evoked strong reactions in India for portraying Hindu deities in the nude. Over the years, Husain was taken to court over the issue many times, and he had even been the target of vandals.

Things got out of hand in 2006 when one of his paintings appeared in a famous Indian magazine. The painting depicted a nude Bharat Mata ("Mother India"). In India, the motherland is often represented as a Hindu goddess.[4] The backlash against the eccentric artist from conservative Indian Hindus was so strong that Husain left India that year and never returned. He became a citizen of Qatar four years later and died the next year in 2011. He was buried in London over fears that his grave would be vandalized in India.

Husain's *Woman at Work*

In 2007, prior to his passing, Husain was awarded the Raja Ravi Varma Award by the government of the southern Indian state of Kerala. The award is named after another famous Indian painter who was also misunderstood in his time. Varma was born in Kerala in 1848 and became famous for re-creating scenes from Hindu mythology using European painting styles. His depictions were revolutionary at the time, and even though he was a Hindu, he was taken to court on charges of blasphemy.[5] Ironically, his portrayal of Hindu deities is now the norm in India. In fact, his new vision of the gods helped shape the modern face of Bharat Mata and even inspired Hindu freedom fighters during India's struggle for independence.

Varma's *Arjuna and Subhadra*

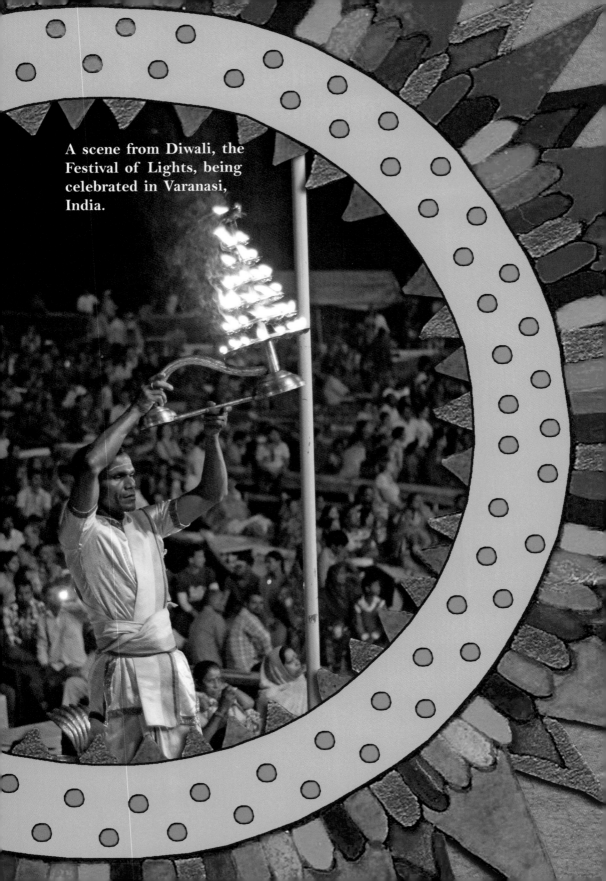

A scene from Diwali, the Festival of Lights, being celebrated in Varanasi, India.

Home for Diwali

Had Dadi already been in the United States for a month? It feels like it was only yesterday when we had picked her up from the Newark Liberty International Airport in New Jersey. I remember it so clearly—my family had been waiting for her to come out of the airport, and my sisters had been the ones to spot her. She had stepped out of the airport in one of her usual white saris behind a porter who was wheeling her luggage.

Now it was time for her to go back to India.

"Dadi, when are you going to visit the United States again?"

Cameron had really taken to my grandmother. He called her by the name that my sisters and I used, and she liked it too. Cameron's grandparents had passed away many years ago when he was very young, and Dadi made him feel like she was his own. She is very fond of him, and when Cameron and I are together, she treats him like her own grandson.

"I don't know when I'll be back, *beta,*" Dadi said to Cameron. "Maybe after a year." She turned to Cameron and wagged one of her gnarly fingers at him. "You must visit me in India soon," she said, and she smiled kindly. My father got his smile from her. She was now packing her suitcases and getting ready for her trip back to India. Cameron had come over to spend time with her. The two of us were with her in her room.

"When are you going to India next?" Cameron asked me.

"Maybe around Diwali. My parents have been talking about taking all of us to Delhi at that time."

"What's Diwali?" Cameron asked.

"It's one of the most important Hindu festivals," I said. "It is also called the Festival of Lights. Do you know why?"

The story of Diwali comes from the Ramayana. Lord Rama had spent fourteen years in exile away from his kingdom in Ayodhya, and when he returned, the people of Ayodhya lit up the whole city with lamps. The lamps symbolized the victory of good over evil, and Hindus all over the world have followed this tradition ever since. That is where the festival gets its name—from *deepavali,* which means "a row of lamps." Fireworks have also become part of Diwali in modern times.

Nine days before Diwali, Hindus celebrate Rama's victory over the evil demon king Ravana during the festival of Dussehra. Diwali itself is celebrated for five days. Some Hindu businesses end their fiscal year on Diwali, and they pray to the goddess Lakshmi for a profitable new year of business. The lamps are also intended to help her find her way into the homes of the devout. Other Hindus trace the origins of Diwali to stories of Krishna or the goddess Kaali.[1]

"When is Diwali, Dadi?" Cameron asked.

"I haven't checked the date for this year, but Diwali usually falls between October and November," she said. "The date keeps changing on the secular calendar because that calendar is based on the sun. The Hindu calendar is based on the sun, the moon, and the stars, all at the same time."[2]

Hindu calendars are prepared by astrologers and astronomers, and they can be very complicated. Hindus even rely on their religious scholars to determine auspicious days and times for important events like weddings, travel, and festivals. There is not a single standard Hindu calendar; they vary by region and local beliefs. Sometimes a festival is celebrated on different days by different Hindus. The most common Hindu calendar is called the Rashtriya Panchang, and it was created by the government of India in 1957.[3] That was also the year they created the Indian National Calendar.

"What about any other Hindu festivals?" Cameron said.

As a religious group, the Hindus possibly celebrate the most number of festivals in the world, and they are all observed with a tremendous amount of color and joy. Some festivals are only observed in certain parts of the world, but in total, they are too many to count. Some historians have estimated Hindu festivals to be in the thousands!

Hindu festivals are usually related to the gods, the family, or the seasons. Holi also has a mythological story related to it, but it is celebrated with the arrival of spring and is also known as the festival of color. Hindus celebrate this festival by throwing colored water and powder on family, friends, and even strangers. During Rakshabandhan, the family takes center stage. Sisters honor their brothers with a decorative thread bracelet, and the brothers return the gesture with presents and a lifelong vow to protect their sisters. Vaishnavites pay special attention to the birthdays of Rama and Krishna, which are called Rama Navami and Krishna Jayanti (or Janmashthami).

A colorful scene from a Holi celebration

"My parents once took me to the Kumbh Mela in Allahabad in India when I was a little girl," Dadi said. "This particular festival occurs once every twelve years at Prayag, which is where the Ganga and Yamuna rivers meet in northern India. I haven't been brave enough to go back—the last time this festival was held in 2013, nearly 100 million people showed up to bathe in the sacred rivers!"[4]

Cameron and I looked at each other in shock. We couldn't imagine so many people gathered in one place. Imagine if all of those people showed up on the shores of the Hudson River—even New York City only has 8.3 million people!

Dadi was amused by our facial expressions. She chuckled as she zipped up her luggage. She had finished packing her belongings, and we only had a couple of hours before she would have to go to the airport to catch her flight to India.

Cameron put his hand in his pocket and walked up to Dadi. "I have a small present for you," he said. He pulled out his hand and opened his palm. "I hope you like it."

Dadi's eyes twinkled as her beautiful face broke out into a smile. "Lord Ganesha," she said softly as she took the small *murti* from Cameron's palm. He had bought her a statue of one of the most recognizable Hindu gods. Ganesha is the son of Shiva and Parvati, and he has the head of an elephant. The Mahabharata is believed to have been dictated to him. Ganesha is the remover of obstacles and symbolizes good luck, which is why many people give his *murti* as a present to friends and travelers. It looks like Cameron had really been reading up about *sanatana dharma*.

"Thank you for spending time with me this past month, Dadi," Cameron said shyly.

Dadi was smiling, but I could see that she was tearing up. She hugged Cameron and kissed him on the top of his head.

"I hope you had a great time in our country," Cameron said. "Please come back soon." He touched Dadi's feet out of respect, the way that Hindus do for their elders. "*Atithi devo bhava,*" he said. The guest is God.

The Evolution Continues

The *Om* symbol represents a holy sound in Hinduism.

Hindu life has changed a lot in the past hundred years. Television and the Internet have displaced scriptures as the primary source of education, and they have brought Western ideas and traditions into Hindu homes.[5] More Hindus now live in nuclear families than ever before, and the ancient *varnashramas* have long been disrupted. Gender roles are particularly undergoing a drastic change. Marriages across *varnas* and even religions are becoming more common.

Varnas, however, still influence daily life. In India, many employers and schools give special consideration to employees and students from lower *varnas*. Certain political parties cater to specific *varnas*, and Hindu parties in general try to retain their footing in religiously diverse countries.

Perhaps the greatest challenge that the Hindus face today is the lack of a united international front. For the first time in Hindu history, its followers can be found in countries all over the world. Hindus who have raised their families in non-Hindu countries worry about their children losing their culture. They feel the need to standardize their beliefs, like the Jews, Christians, and Muslims, who have fixed dogmas and rituals. These religions began with a definite creed that gave rise to many sects over time. *Sanatana dharma* has been the opposite—it was loosely scattered across the hearts and minds of individuals for most of its history, but maybe the time has come for one central Hindu creed. Others worry that codifying Hindu beliefs will rob them of their essence.

Another symbol of Hinduism is the Hindu swastika which represents Brahman.

BCE

c. 2,500–1,500	The Indus Valley Civilization flourishes in northwestern India.
c. 1,500–500	The Vedic Period: Aryans arrive in South Asia; the Vedas are compiled.
c. 1,000–300	The Brahmanas and Upanishads are composed.
c. 500 BCE–500 CE	The Ramayana and the Mahabharata are composed. The worship of *murtis* (statues) and of Vishnu, Shiva, and Shakti becomes popular. Buddhism and Jainism become popular.
327	Alexander the Great invades India.
322–182	The Mauryan Empire unites much of India.
c. 300 BCE–300 CE	The Sangam literature, the earliest known Tamil literature, is compiled.
c. 200	Temples are built in caves. The *varnas* are codified in the scriptures.
c. 150	The Bhagavad Gita is composed.

CE

320–550	The reign of the Gupta Dynasty. Hindu culture becomes dominant with the construction of numerous monuments and temples.
500–1000	The Bhakti movement takes place in southern India. Poet-saints compose devotional poems in Tamil.
535–700	The Harsha Empire unites northern India.
800–1200	The peak of temple construction in southern India.
1000	Raids are conducted in India by the Afghan Muslim Mahmud of Ghaznavi.
1010–1200	South India's Chola Empire extends Hinduism into Southeast Asia.
c. 1140	The temple complex of Angkor Wat is built in Cambodia.
1200–1500	Muslim merchants and missionaries settle in Southeast Asia.
1469	Guru Nanak, the founder of Sikhism, is born.
1486	The saint Chaitanya Mahaprabhu is born.
1498	Portuguese explorer Vasco da Gama arrives in India. Christian missionaries follow in his path.
1526–1857	The Mughal Empire rules in India.
1600s	European traders arrive in India for cloth and spices.
1750	India falls under the control of the British East India Company.
1828	Raja Ram Mohan Roy and Debendrenath Tagore start the Brahmo Samaj reform society.
1830	Hindus begin to migrate to Fiji, Malaysia, Mauritius, the Caribbean, East Africa, and South Africa.
1856	Widow remarriage becomes legal in India.
1857	The British suppress a combined Hindu-Muslim rebellion in northern India.
1858	India becomes part of the British Empire.

1869	Mohandas Karamchand Gandhi is born.
1875	Swami Dayananad Saraswati founds the Arya Samaj reform movement.
1877	Queen Victoria becomes the Empress of India.
1895	Swami Vivekananda founds the Vedanta Society.
1914–1918	World War I.
1915	Gandhi joins the Indian independence movement.
1920–1922	Gandhi's civil disobedience campaign.
1925	The Rashtriya Swayamsevak Sangh (RSS) is founded in India as a Hindu nationalist group.
1939–1945	World War II.
1942	Gandhi starts the "Quit India" movement.
1947	India, East Pakistan (later Bangladesh), and West Pakistan (later Pakistan) are created from British India.
1948	Gandhi is assassinated by a Hindu nationalist. India and Pakistan battle over Kashmir.
1950	India becomes a republic with the introduction of its constitution.
1950s–1970s	Hindus migrate to the United States, the United Kingdom, and other countries, such as Holland and Australia.
1960s	Indian thought and practice becomes popular in the West, through groups such as the Transcendental Meditation and ISKCON.
1962	India goes to war with China over border issues.
1965	India's second war with Pakistan over Kashmir.
1970	Acharya Rajneesh starts the Osho movement.
1971	India and Pakistan wage war over East Pakistan (now Bangladesh).
1984	The Indian Prime Minister Indira Gandhi is assassinated by Sikh separatists. Hindu-Sikh riots ensue.
1992	The demolition of a mosque in Ayodhya, India, by a Hindu mob leads to Hindu-Muslim violence across the country.
1999	India fights its fourth war with Pakistan in Kargil, Kashmir.
2000	Strife continues between Christians and Hindus over coerced religious conversions in parts of India.
2002	Hindu-Muslim clashes in Gujarat kill thousands.
2008	Pakistani gunmen attack Mumbai in India.
2013	Pilgrims die in a stampede during the Maha Kumbh Mela in Allahabad, India.
2014	An Indus Valley era stepwell is found in Dholavari, India, that is three times larger than the Great Bath in Mohenjo-daro, Pakistan.

Chapter Notes

Chapter 1. New Jersey Hindus

1. Jeaneane Fowler, *Hinduism—Beliefs and Practices* (Portland, Oregon: Sussex Academic Press, 1997), pp. 17–18.
2. Pew Research Religion & Public Life Project: The Global Religious Landscape—Hindus, http://www.pewforum.org/2012/12/18/global-religious-landscape-hindu/
3. Rasamandala Das, *The Illustrated Encyclopedia of Hinduism* (Leicester, UK: Anness Publishing, 2012), pp. 194–195.
4. John Bowker, *World Religions* (New York: DK Publishing, 2003), pp. 42–43.
5. Pew Research Religion & Public Life Project.

Chapter 2. All Roads Lead To India

1. Rasamandala Das, *The Illustrated Encyclopedia of Hinduism* (Leicester, UK: Anness Publishing, 2012), pp. 6–7.
2. Steven J. Rosen, *Essential Hinduism* (Westport, Connecticut: Praeger Publishers, 2006), p. 24.
3. Ibid, p. 2.
4. Das, pp. 148–151.
5. Linda Johnsen, *The Complete Idiot's Guide to Hinduism* (New York: Alpha Books, 2009), pp. 19–32.

Chapter 3. One Soul, Many Lives

1. Steven J. Rosen, *Essential Hinduism* (Westport, Connecticut: Praeger Publishers, 2006), p. xix.
2. Jeaneane Fowler, *Hinduism—Beliefs and Practices* (Portland, Oreg.: Sussex Academic Press, 1997), pp. 19–24.
3. Rosen, p. xiv.
4. Ibid, pp. 151–167.
5. Fowler, pp. 61–62.

Chapter 4. Hindus in History

1. Rosen, Steven J. *Essential Hinduism* (Westport, Connecticut: Praeger Publishers, 2006), pp. 21–25.
2. Das, Rasamandala. *The Illustrated Encyclopedia of Hinduism* (Leicester, UK: Anness Publishing, 2012), pp. 234–235.
3. Ibid, p. 35.
4. Ibid, pp. 140–141.
5. Raghu Karnad, "For the Love of the Gods," *Tehelka,* August 30, 2008, http://archive.tehelka.com/story_main40.asp?filename=hub230808fortheloveofthegods.asp

Chapter 5. Home for Diwali

1. Jeaneane Fowler, *Hinduism—Beliefs and Practices* (Portland, Oregon: Sussex Academic Press, 1997), pp. 70–71.
2. Steven J. Rosen, *Essential Hinduism* (Westport, Connecticut: Praeger Publishers, 2006), pp. 207–208.
3. Ibid.
4. Saibal Chatterjee, "Kumbh Mela Documentary Makes Waves in Toronto," *BBC News,* September 19, 2013, http://www.bbc.co.uk/news/world-asia-india-24125635
5. Rasamandala Das, *The Illustrated Encyclopedia of Hinduism* (Leicester, UK: Anness Publishing, 2012), pp. 188–189.

Books

365 Tales from Indian Mythology. NOIDA, India: Om Books International, 2006.

Arni, Samahita. *Sita's Ramayana.* Toronto: Groundwood Books, 2011.

Gokhale, Namita. *The Puffin Mahabharata.* New Delhi: Viking (India), 2009.

Jani, Mahendra, and Vandana Jani. *What You Will See Inside a Hindu Temple.* Woodstock, Vermont: Skylight Paths Publishing, 2005.

Works Consulted

Bowker, John. *World Religions.* New York: DK Publishing, 2003.

Dalrymple, William. *Nine Lives—In Search of the Sacred in Modern India.* New York: Alfred A. Knopf, 2009.

Das, Rasamandala. *The Illustrated Encyclopedia of Hinduism.* Leicester, UK: Anness Publishing, 2012.

Fowler, Jeaneane. *Hinduism—Beliefs and Practices.* Portland, OR: Sussex Academic Press, 1997.

Freeman, Michael, and Claude Jacques. *Ancient Angkor.* Bangkok, Thailand: River Books, 2012.

Johnsen, Linda. *The Complete Idiot's Guide to Hinduism.* New York: Alpha Books, 2009.

Rosen, Steven J. *Essential Hinduism.* Westport, CT: Praeger Publishers, 2006.

On the Internet

BBC: Religions—Hinduism
 http://www.bbc.co.uk/religion/religions/hinduism/
International Society for Krishna Consciousness (ISKCON)
 http://iskcon.org/
Sanskrita Pradipika
 http://www.sanskrit-lamp.org
Srimad Bhagavad-Gita
 http://www.bhagavad-gita.org/

astrologer (as-TRAW-luh-jer)—Someone who predicts the future by the positions of the planets, sun, and moon.

astronomer (as-TRAW-nuh-mer)—A scientific observer of the heavenly bodies.

auspicious (aw-SPIH-shus)—Favored by fortune.

betrothal (beh-TROH-thal)—Engagement to be married.

blasphemy (BLAS-fem-ee)—An act of disrespecting God.

codify (KOH-dih-fy)—To arrange according to a system.

colonize (KAW-luh-nize)—To subject a population to a colonial government.

consciousness (KAWN-shus-ness)—The state or condition of being conscious.

consort (KON-sort)—A companion or partner.

cosmic (KAHZ-mik)—Relating to the whole universe.

creed (KREED)—A written body of teaching of a religious group.

cremate (KREE-mayt)—To reduce to ash by fire.

debris (deb-REE)—The fragments or remnants of something destroyed.

dogma (DOG-ma)—A doctrine or code of beliefs accepted as authoritative.

downtrodden (DOWN-traw-den)—Oppressed.

eccentric (ek-SEN-trik)—Unusual.

enlightenment (en-LAI-ten-ment)—A blessed state in which the individual transcends desire and suffering.

epic (EH-pik)—A long narrative poem telling of a hero's deeds.

exile (EG-zyl)—The act of expelling a person from his or her native land.

fiscal (FIS-kal)—Relating to finance.

front (FRUNT)—A group of people with common ideas who try to achieve certain goals.

glacier (GLAY-sher)—A slowly moving mass of ice.

incarnation (in-kar-NAY-shun)—Time passed in a particular bodily form.

indentured (in-DEN-tured)—Bound by contract; working to pay a debt.

intoxicant (in-TOK-sih-kint)—Any substance that creates in a person a state ranging from euphoria to stupor, usually accompanied by loss of inhibitions and control.

linguist (LIN-guist)—A person who studies foreign languages.

mainstream (MAYN-streem)—The prevailing current of thought.

mythology (mih-THAW-luh-jee)—A collection of myths or stories.

nomadic (NOH-mad-ik)—A person of no fixed residence.

pantheon (PAN-thee-awn)—All the gods of a religion.

pilgrimage (PIL-grim-ej)—A journey to a sacred place.

reincarnation (ree-in-kar-NAY-shun)—Rebirth of a soul in another body.

renunciate (ree-NUN-see-et)—Someone who gives up material life and lives in isolation.

retreat (reh-TREET)—A place or period of withdrawal for prayer, meditation, or study.

rite of passage—Any act or event marking a passage from one stage of life to another.

secular (SEK-yoo-lur)—Not concerned with religion.

shrine—A container or receptacle for sacred relics.

standardize (STAN-der-dyz)—To cause to conform to a standard or norm.

trinity (TRIH-nih-tee)—A group consisting of three closely related members.

trivialize (TRIH-vee-uh-lyz)—To cause to appear unimportant.

tyrant (TY-runt)—A cruel and oppressive ruler.

vandal (VAN-dul)—Someone who willfully destroys property.

Index

Khadija Ejaz is an internationally published and translated poet and the author of several books. She was born in Lucknow, India, raised in Muscat, Oman, and has also lived in Toronto, Canada, and New Delhi, India. Khadija now lives in the United States, where she earned her undergraduate and graduate degrees in information technology. She has also worked in broadcast journalism at New Delhi Television and dabbles in filmmaking and photography. To learn more about Khadija, visit her web site at http://khadijaejaz.netfirms.com.